POEMS BY ERIKA GARZA-JOHNSON

FLOWERSONG BOOKS
AN IMPRINT OF
VAO PUBLISHING

DONNA, TX

ISBN 10: 0692323902
ISBN 13: 978-0692323908

FlowerSong Books
An imprint of VAO Publishing
A division of Valley Artistic Outreach
4717 N FM 493
Donna, TX 78537
www.vaopublishing.com

First printed edition: December 2014

Contents

DETACHABLE VENUS

every day
a goddess falls apart

as Barbie loses her head
Cihuacoatl can't find her cry
and Ixtaccihuatl
fell out of the arms of a
dismembered hero
unaware of her peril

every day another
goddess can't find her wings
and all those things that make
her who she is

Coatlicue just can't
keep herself together
She's a mess!

Venus found her hairpiece
in the garbage heap of man

and Cihuateotl lost Cihuateteo
displacing duality once more

#LAMERAMERAMETAPOEM

There is a canvas HEB bag filled with my poems. I keep them in
my office. Some days I hear them praying. Benditos poemas.
Sometimes I hear one of them chant. Like a Gregorian monk.
Once a poem reminded me to wash the towels. Household chores
disturb my sleep. (I know my home is disheveled and I don't have
the attention span to clean.) The poems talk about how I used to
be a slut. They talk behind my back, I know they do. One of
them laughed at her line breaks. It was a Tuesday. I turned the
window unit on because it was 102 degrees and it gets stuffy for
them inside my tote bag. "Don't you ever want to be read?" I
asked one of them. "No. We want to sit here in this bag until you
die." I chuckled. Silly poems. Tomorrow, I think, will mark some
kind of anniversary, but I am not sure. I think it's probably
because I wrote a poem about being a holiday. I know that I lost
poems many moves ago. One time, I left a binder of them on a
bench and when I came back it was gone. The poems probably
sucked anyway. I promise never to leave any of my poems behind
again.

RIO GRANDE

how do you steal your own memory
mimic your own voice
write something
without
writing
about it

"Pues esas cosas no se dicen"

so I've sealed
my own heart away
and sent it to silencio
ripped my hands off
erased my face and
drowned my past in the
Rio Grande
I cross it back
this cross on my back
and deny myself the freedom
to dance

I have forgotten rhythm

so clumsily I fall
back in to the
Rio Grande
and wet

have gone home to
black out pictures

so no one knows my ancestors

Poem Written While Grading

1. To break bread with schizophrenics, you must not speak in tongues.
2. At least one apostle had dissociative identity disorder.
3. There is always one friend in your group who is like Judas.
4. If it had been one last brunch instead of a last supper, would the Bloody Marys be blessed?
5. Blasphemy tastes bitter to atheists.
6. He was an award winning crucifix maker, made them in record breaking time.
7. Jesucristo hums alabanzas while blessing prostitutes.
8. She made an accidental horcrux when she aborted the rapist's child.
9. All over my home town: stations-of-the-cross pop up like drive-thrus.
10. Decoy deer dressed for Christmas and has nowhere to go.

BARRIDA

I need a barrida.
Get rid of my susto.
Ramas del cedro
y un credo.
Sueño sueños pendejos.
A baby in a white onesie
clawing me.
A tattooed man I whisper lies to--
lies that burn my lips.
I dream of dreams that make me feel alive.
More than this.
I feel like a wound.
Una herida with a beating feverish tenderness.
A wound that cannot, will not,
does not know how to heal.
I am a wound.
Memories of purple blue bruises.
Memories of bloody noses.
Memories of fantasies and false hopes.
Memories of men I've used, women.
Memories of memories and all I am
is womb of more memories.
I dream I will be flesh again.
Brown skin.
Bright eyed.
Long curly hair.

Woman with breasts, ass, soft thighs.
Woman with passion.
Woman with healed wounds.
Woman again.

WHAT I WORE

If you must know
It was a black satin kilt
A silver baby tee
Black patent maryjanes
Glitter lotion that smelled of plumeria

If you must know
It was a flowery dress
Knee length
Knee high socks
White platforms

If you must know
I wore cut off shorts
Sequined tank top
Flip flops

If you must know
I don't remember
what I was wearing

All I remember
is that he promised to take me home.
He promised me if I told anyone he would kill me.
If I told anyone no one would believe me.
Because I was Mexican.
Because I was too poor to afford a lawyer.
He told me I would ruin his marriage—
What about his children?

I wore warmups for days
I only went out in pantsuits
I wore penny loafers and button down oxfords
I never went out again

If you must know
I took that night
crumpled it up into a ball
and burned it in the oil drum
my father used to burn trash.

Fan the flames.
Fill the winter night
with ashes.

To Be Honest

I'm gonna go kill my muse
I am not looking for a new one
This muse is manic
This muse is ugly
This muse has a horse face
She has no reflection
She is the ghost of a dead poem
I have seen her eyeing another
Cabrona
Sometimes she catches me in the middle of a poem and tries to
strangle me
This muse is infatuated with clichés
She wants to rhyme long, song, bong,
Ding dong the muse is dead!
Bury the muse
Bury her words, her impulses, her leaping
Bury the muse
Place plastic flowers on her grave
A corona from a yerbería

I don't need a muse

I need a tourniquet

LABELED

This is my label
I removed it off a can of refried beans
Here's my label
Peeled off of Juanita's Menudo in a can, Man!

My label
Peeled off a box of Marias

Recycle my label
Burn my label
My label sticks to your shoes
My soul a label
My hair a label
Unlabeled
This label a fable
The label on the table for others to discuss
Roundtable

I'm sick of labels
Of misunderstood peoples
Of victims
Of sickness
Of mental illness
Of missing opportunities
Because I dread labels
Because I dread being mislabeled
Because I dread being only a label

Untitled

never make love to a poet
you will awake touching your breasts
not recognizing them
and look in the mirror into eyes
that are not yours
your visage that of a violated nun

never make love to a poet
you will remember unrequited kisses
and words you will spit
your tongue thick
never make love to a poet
you will no longer have a soul
once he has rewritten it

PINCHE PRINCESS

Because so many girls believe
they are royalty
and mothers and marketers
encourage this delusion
of pink ponies, plastic heels,
feather boas, ball gowns, tiaras…
I shop for my little girl
and am attacked by pink and lavender.
Everywhere.

I would much rather shop for my little boy
who could be a rockstar,
any variety of athlete, a paleontologist,
entomologist, a race car driver, train engineer,
robot scientist…
And my unborn girl is a pinche princess.
Y a lo mejor, si Dios quiere,
a slutty pop star.

Since birth we convince our
girls they must stay clean,
play clean, wear feathered slippers,
heels at two (although they are still learning to walk),
sit properly, their little legging clad legs crossed
at proper princess tea parties
wearing gowns and our boys
are little savages and it's O.K.
Because they are boys.
Because they are boys.

Chicana moms make excuses for their little boys
who mess up their lives
and all they get is a
ay, pobrecito mi'jito.

Pregnant teen princesses—dressing
their baby girls in little pink clothes
perpetuating pinche princess futures
without a prince.

Brown in the Wrong Town

I often feel unwoven.

I know the landscape of my dreams
filled with images of my once home
but now I search and try to memorize
the unknown.

I have tried to weave myself again
wear my new heart
this huipil that suits me
for the woman I have become.

Mujer.
Madre.
Esposa.

But I can't stay under the radar.
Brown in the wrong town.
Barrio in the suburbs
rascuache to the core
but why should anyone
know that I grew up poor?

I have tried to assimilate
wear my head on as straight as I can
or at least, my costume appears to be such
that while I am Mexican in my blood

No one needs to know.

MUSING

We slept with a gun in our bed.
In plain view.
Not under a pillow.
You kept it right next to your hand,
with a finger by the trigger.

This is how we spent every night.
You wore paisley. Silk.
We were in a cartel.
We smuggled kittens
and they would sell for hundreds of dollars.

You were speaking to me in a voice
that wasn't yours.

I wasn't sure what to do with the cats.
They were restless.

Birds were migrating today.
Cormorants, snow geese, a few falcons,
a herring, what was that bird?

Later we went to Delta Lake and it was empty.
No more water in the lake just skeletons.
At the pavilion danced
an old man wearing python boots.
He cursed at us.

"¡Pinches gatos!" he yelled.
It was just you and I and the old man
who may have been Bukowksi.

How young was I then?
What came of it all?

I am having a hard time
today because all
I want to do is take care of you.

Bar Poems

1.

Excuses are not meant to be kept like promises.

Harbor resentment and harvest regret.

Would it have been well spent?

If my memories acculturate—
language is lost.

2.

Measure heartbeat like moon dew
and what if the sun rises into oblivion?
Joan Didion?

If cancer persists, what is resist?
Life should end in an exclamation point,
and what of the semi-colon?

Epitaphs poorly written without punctuation.

Tell them I said—hello.

NATURALLY

Woke up one morning
and my sweet potato vine
was gone.
My calonchoes
hit the road
along with my livingstone daisies,
corona de cristo,
my lucky ébano, hackberrry, ash trees,
all the lengua-de-suegra,
the rosemary, the piñata lavender,
even my variegated hibiscus
peach and red plate booms forever missing
from my front window view.

Nothing was left
only the fire pit
filled with white ashes
and sweet mesquite pods
for me to burn to remember
winter nights,
to remember I had blue moon roses,
afterglow succulent,
a sweet memory of a sunset framed
with the cactus now stolen.

and She, guiltily
reading her poetry

with evidence of thorns on her palms.

Mariposas Muertas

Why do I drink?

When I recall what you said
I just want to cry

You know,
about how the butterflies died.

It's a tragedy, bring out
a violin, an accordion,
break out the canned beer.

Why do I drink?

Why
am
I sitting
here
drinking?

Because the butterflies
had a funeral in my belly.

They won't flutter again.
I won't feel that je ne sais quoi

Just burp dead butterflies.

What an affair to forget.

Rapture Chachalacas

The chachalacas sang an ominous song this morning.
A shifty-eyed chachalaca called out to me.
I said "Hold on now" as I swept the patio.
¡Híjole! Chachalacas are impatient.

Have you ever listened to their song?
If you reverse it they are calling God.
God is busy.
Not for chachalacas.

This morning was an oven that smelled like nalgas.

Cleaned out the washing machine.
Creepy cross-eyed chachalaca in the window
scraped the glass with a crooked claw.
I count change to buy some smokes.

Chacha (I named the shifty eyed one, for fun) followed me to the
Smoke Shop.
Chacha and the cross-eyed one are married.
Turnio (crossed eyes) is a cheat.
Cheating chachalacas. That ain't right.

KISS was at Starbucks by the Smoke Shop.
It is said when the painted ones order
toasted coconut mocha frappucino the world will end.

Lit a Gunsmoke and walked back home.
Suicide sticks. Taste like the apocalypse.
It's already noon. Chacha needed a nap. Missing
her children. She looks at me, gray feathers molting.

Chachalacas and chores on this day before the world ends.

Third Street

My barrio is a pool of tears
that should be tested for pollutants that
cause cancer of the

blood I shed contaminated with chemicals
from old sheds that produced plastics

uplifted railroad tracks sold for scrap so
town could pay its debt to pick up trash

my barrio is a cesspool of dreams born from
a cesarean section
with muscles yet to heal

the barrio is not where i belong
it is my source of sufrimiento
sadness of wilted corpses

my barrio flew away
in a bubble i blew
when my niece was two

my barrio does not have jazz
but out the window framed with
rotted wood
two huskies fuck
in an abandoned lot

Paletero at Midnight

delivers beersicles.
Chicharrones con cholula.
He knows your vicios.
Micheladas, mangonadas
he's got what you need.
Sometimes Xanax.
Paletero at midnight does not honk his horn
and awaken the children.
When he is near you, you know.
He is part brujo.
If you are an insomniac,
he'll even deliver a dream.

MAYAHUEL

The leaves fall off and the tree blooms, at once.
Abortion silences an artist.
Her photos delete
themselves.
We bathe in mud
while we bloodlet.
The aborted fetus
comes back as a clear winged butterfly.

We would name her Mayahuel.

Spring time and she would dance
in the piñata lavender. Pollinate.

A luminaria for the nights of drogas sucias.
Luminaria by the bedside of carelessness.
A luminaria, glowing embryo who lets out
a myopic sigh. Mayahuel.

We toast you with Guzano Rojo
as the mala mujer simmers on the stove

KILN

Hear. Here is your rib and your iPod.
I borrowed them with the intention
of seeing you again. I keep a transparent
plastic box filled with items I stole
from you that night when we mixed
raw ocher and cobalt oxide.

The kiln was ablaze and we smoked Pall Malls.
I borrowed your hoodie even though I was sweating.

Every night I kiss the shrapnel
you saved from a war you never fought.

Promesas to the Dead

If this northern wind could stop time
I'd hug you
Embrace your fragility

I would be a miracle worker

I would erase
I would suspend
I would mend
I would be illogical
I would hear you breathe, again
We would harmonize
As we sang alabanzas
No one would ever doubt hope
No one would ever die
And we would always pray

ILL EAGLES

Sick birds who can't fly away from their own fate
Who do fly but land in broken nests
Who are sent back
After their painful dangerous migration
Who are locked away in cold cages
Whose wings are clipped
Who are forced to work
Who forget their cry
Who once represented
The majesty of flight and freedom
Only to be shot down while they dream

FOLK TELL

1.
No one in a dingy dress in duress
roamed around drainage ditches.

It's what she hadn't said.
It's that her children,
whom she had not killed,
starved to death from malnourishment.

It's not that her husband was unfaithful or left,
but died in the desert of delusion.

It's that her uterus was overrun by cancerous polyps
and she had no insurance.
Her babies were never born.

2.
The Llorona cries in her fluorescent lit office,
straining to see her dim Dell screen.
She has checked her android phone
no one has called her in days.

She is tired of taking the blame.
She has no intention of taking the blame.
She wants to turn her tears into words.

Words
not
tears

meant to flow,
to become song.

A floricanto of forgiveness
and revolution.

Agua Bendita

Drinking holy water does not cure cancer.
Do not chug it.
It will not get rid of Diabetes, High Blood Pressure,
Cirrhosis, Psoriasis, Eczema, Edema.
Holy water on your joints
will not ease the Rheumatoid Arthritis,
although, I have heard (and believe) that cannabis
in a jar of baby oil, a lo mejor, pero,
maybe just smoke it y sóbate bien.
Agua bendita works better when poured
on the baby when she is fussy,
or the little boy who will not calm down,
"¡Parece que tiene un demonio!"

Holy water does not cure cancer.
Education and prevention and hope.

Hope and holy water may help.

Sprinkle both and call me in the morning.

HOMESICK

what happens if the flower vendor's rebozo
comes undone and her children
spill out on the muddy street
and what happens if
the toothless abuelita's styrofoam cup is bottomless
her coins float off into the infinite
what happens if the tacos run out
beer runs out
the limes are hard
avocadoes are watery and never ripen
what happens if the tourists finally stop acting like jerks
what if they never stay down here for the winter
never want another pewter cross
or a mariachi hat
what if the .925 silver tarnishes in the wind
the accordion tunes itself
the scorpions in the polyresin belt buckle sting
again and the margaritas are made with freon

what if i never get to visit my border town again?

INSTRUCTIONS

leave clichés at the door
you will find a box full of trite ideas
flowery language
sexual spanish
overly celebrated overused metaphors
recycled llantos
abuelas

there in that box
folktales retold too many times
they have lost their precautionary element
canciones sung drunkenly
and danced to since high school

in summation
breathe
through the noise
don't yell poems
preach nothing

throw away a saint
effigies are piñatas for political pachangas
charanga backwards
manaeds murmur secrets
hidden in couch cushions
remove wreaths off doors
covered in robins' eggs
re-cover the mirrors
sit down to watch novelas based on your own life

in summation
if on occasion
you must remind yourself
who you are

rid of your misery
remain a mystery

don't forget to tip your bartender

STILL

sometimes i feel spring suffocate me
and my silver wings static.

stifling, this shift. stifling, my sorrow.
stifling, the silt, the salt, the savage
sad. the plain is empty. the barren.

the bliss, is?

this i missed.

when it rained
the sun shined on us.
the rain shined.
the rain was a shiny thing
and we danced and laughed
with a baby vampire
and drank hard lemonade.

the sad is savage and my heart
gun powder. a bullet i shot you.

the bitter bad
bruised bitch with an
arrow in her
back.

OFFICE CANTO

Today is a quiet day that yells in my ears.
Too much silence and I feel the suture.
Ghosts hum louder than the buzz of the lights.
They shuffle the papers I haven't graded.
I hide under the desk and crawl into the portal of my past.
But all I can see is the future.

CIRRUS CLOUDS, SUNSET

His eyes, the sky.
My heart, the color of ditch water.
My lungs will not let me run.
The helicopter circles these days.
War sound.
War sound.
A war sound of chicharras vs. cucarachos.
I worry for the fat man who says "No!"
to his dog but won't wave "Hello."
I feel for his pale wife who has four shih tzus
and is afraid of my children.
That's none of my business.
I try to exercise, exorcise my shadow,
my memories yet to exist,
my children who grow up too fast.
I'm in the business of yanking off yellow
trumpet flowers to send to God.
The sun is sinking into the cirrus clouds.
Goodbye to this day.
Goodbye to your eyes.

FREAK STORM

Lately there are no seasons here.
Freak hail storm came stole the blossoms and leaves
off the flowers and trees
even though it is 95 degrees
it looks like winter in mid Spring.

There are no seasons here.

We drive through the neighborhood
see the damaged windows covered in cardboard
plywood our own windows
mosquitos creep in
and I unwish rain.
There are no seasons here.

It's an insult to read of snow.
Snow is salt.
Salt on this wound where there is no winter
where winter scraped me.
There is a shadow that winter left
yet there is no shade.

There are no seasons here.

For one day the seasons met
a tornado touched down
tore shingles off roofs
snapped the sunflowers
stole yellow esperanza blooms

yellow huisache blooms
white wild olive blooms
shredded the cacti
stole my dad's bamboo
the plant I gave him his last father's day.

The neighbor died last week.
Her body was cremated.
Her house is alone.
Her garden is gone.

There are no seasons here.

BEDTIME STORY FOR INSOMNIACS

Once upon a time
There was a woman named Ache.
Her very core was pain.

She had been made
with the bones
of her ancestors.

Every night
she sacrificed herself.

Her penance:
three our fathers,
one hail mary,
pulque.

Her imaginary friend was Insomnia.
They held hands or played jacks.

Once in a while they would play
shadow puppets with a tall, dark, faceless
man named Valentin.
He wore a black guayabera.

By its very nature
light is loud.

Don't you remember revolution?

Imprisoned
by fear
we can still sing.

Urraca Song

1.

I was told I could not receive the Holy Eucharist
because I was not married by the Catholic Church.
I forgave the priest.

I was told my marriage
does not exist in the eyes of God.

My daughter is my baby girl.
She prefers her father.

Sometimes I sneak into my son's
room and watch him sleep
because I miss him already.

Time, irreversible continuum,
crap.

2.

I want to be an urraca.

Tomorrow I will visit the
witchcraft/goth clothing/incense/
stripper lingerie/shoe store/yerbería
for black wings made from grackle feathers.

I'll wear them as I stare open-mouthed at the dry sky.

I'll wear them as I write
letters to the Father, Son, Holy Ghost
asking for forgiveness.

I'll wear them as I fly
from my treehouse
to the bus stop

I'll wear them as I ride the bus that takes me to work.

When I get there I will take off my wings
fold them nice and neat
place them in my tote-bag
and lecture about rhetorical analysis.

As I write on the eraser board
one lone feather
will fall to the floor.

CORAZÓN ARREPENTIDO

Today my heart was a river.
I cried out my memories.
As it rained
the frogs
escaped.
I watched my toddler play
holding a black umbrella
and heard a corpse
weep in a cement casket.

VENAS/VENTANAS

1.

In this vein
Blame

Tonight he will snore
the children will find their way
Into our room
On to the bed
I'll dream of demons
Of enemies who made me write poems

I'd say blame erases art
Rumors freeze time
Lechuzas scratch at windows
My subconscious betrays me

Blame
In this vein
Shame
In this regret but never forget

Memory is not blood
Here's my home in planet reminisce
Off nostalgia lane
But I've been blamed again

2.

What should I wear to my funeral?
Will you guys come?

In this vein
Your song. Your eyes.
I've bloodlet again
They whispered and I eavesdropped

I must go paint my face
Porque soy descarada

Once

if i could distill blood,
reverse osmosis plasma,
purify memories
and siphon all these impurities
the intoxicants i swallow on a daily basis
to digest the pain, to cope,
all this silt from the past,

expunge secrets,
blow unrequited passion into a paper
bag and watch it float,

set these cells free to fly off into infinity

would you
finally release me?

Or will the crumbs of your había una vez
always bring me back?

YOUR NAME WILL BE EARTH

My problem is I have a temper. My life is a temper tantrum that I didn't throw because I was hiding in the closet. I was hiding in the closet, under the table, afraid to say anything. I didn't want to say anything. There crawls a cockroach. There is no more Raid. I kill my sins.

My problem is the world is ending every day and I am homesick. I am homesick and all I think about is you. I live with these 2 cent sins and there is no confession. God is dead. God died in 2012. We buried him, we buried her. Bury me. I am still alive but I can't breathe. I can't catch my breath. Today feels like a good die to get a tattoo. Your name will be on my arm forever. That way you will die with me. Your name will be Earth.

My problem is I can't stand fluorescent light anymore. I can't stand up to the pain anymore. I want to drink every night to leave the pain. To leave my brain. I don't recognize my face. I don't recognize my children. I don't feel like skin and bones anymore. I feel like ocean. I feel like river water. I feel fluid and fluid is free. Fluidity is freedom. I can't swim.

My problem is there are people who want to live. They want to see tomorrow and tomorrow seems sweet. Their middle name is Hope. They pray. They believe in heaven. They treat each other with respect. They have dignity. They are responsible. They don't fold clothes when they are drunk. They don't fantasize about smothering themselves. They don't have panic attacks in their office and want to scream fire in a hallway so everyone will go home. Someone right now is dying in a hospital bed. Someone right now is sitting down for the last time and they are staring out of a hospital window wishing they could walk outside once more. Someone is enjoying their last meal, savoring life one last time. And all I can think about is how hell feels like living sometimes.

PANADERÍA PERDIDA

There is a trail of mollete
crumbs I've followed
to a July afternoon
spent in my mom's house
hanging with my nieces
little girls who want nothing
more than to color
and play with me.

The trail leads me back to my
father sipping instant coffee
reading National Geographic out loud
or sharing stories of his years spent in Korea.

My mother watching *Primer Impacto*—
"A ver qué desgracias pasaron."
We wait for Walter Mercado's mucho amor.

When I still had a skinny body
filled with youth and agility
petty worry
without knowledge that one day

I would stand in my dirty kitchen
following a sour dough crumb
trail that leads
to their absence.

LA CHINGONA WANNA-BE

I am a vixen.
A woman with a heart of
silky stone,
smooth semi-precious earthen mineral.
Whose eyes have seen,
body felt
lust love passion hate –
all at once.

A head turner,
eye catcher,
attention getter,
I slither in pleather,
bring two brothers to rival.

I cannot only
control you
but
destroy you
and love you with the strength of oak.
Superglue you to my breasts,
make your once tidy world a mess.
Yes.
A vixen,
temptress,
dominatrix.

Si hombre.

A nerd with a pen and too much time on her hands.

Poetic.
Pathetic.

UNDERWORLD

There's no crawling anymore
It's more of a cruise ship
Full amenities y todo
With a view of pestilence
Through the circular window
Like Love Boat but better
Chillin' in Xibalba
Oh yeah
I got the full paid one-way cruise
And every night a new show
All you can drink,
Buffet, lo que sea——
Gambling after dusk
Watching a projected sunset
Sipping micheladas on the deck
Every night a new dark room or cave
New tests
Can I keep the room lit with a cigarette?
Or will the bats finally kill me?
Puro *Popul Vuh* style
But I'm a heroine without a twin
Or a hymen
And the spittle in my hands
Does not belong to you
It's mine and alone
Without a child to remake the world
I sail through the underworld
In search of death without success.

PANTHEON PLAYGROUND

Vamos a bailar.
Hallemos la orisha que nos pertenece.
We can beat the batá,
Learn the rhythm of the Obatala, Yemaya—
Let's exist in another universe.
We'll have a pantheon playground.
Ignore the x-box that refuses DVD's,
Ignore the booted Pasat in the the parking lot.
Let's dance,
Divining all night.
Do we know our future?
No.
Let's throw coconut shells
On the ground and see how they land,

What they say.
No estamos solos.
Tenemos el divino de nosotros,
And the spirits we will meet.
Let them mount us.
Or—
Let's just mount each other.

VOIDS

voids are not parades.
yet they cannot help but honk and
the pomp is hard to leave at home.
alone. in darkness. you kidding me?
all this nothing for no one to share with?

voids often cast a shadow at midnight
they do not like to be tickled
stay clear of them
if they decide to rummage through chests filled with
Happy Meal toys.
they can be finicky when asked about
what it is they want for dinner.

voids like hopscotch.

voids should stay away from fireworks
and gossamer gowns and dyed violet
satin pumps.
voids should never under any circumstance,
decorate cakes, gather tokens
or see the light of electronic games and carousels.

voids should cut hearts out of old calendars with children
at home when the weather looks grim and
swallow tears into the abyss that
once could have played with happiness.

AFTER READING LA SYLVIA PLATH

I erased all the sadness
That I read yesterday
But it rewrote itself
On my tearoom yellow
Walls. Graffiti in the kitchen
Tattooing in sprayed ink,
A flayed cat.
The sadness turned into
Anger not even the alcohol
Could undo, undo, black shoe
Living like a broken toe.
Sadness. The graphite pencil shades
Itself. A still-life of rotting grapefruits.
Puddle of furry puppies,
Mangy messes that yelp.
Try to erase something permanent.
Blood on the pavement——
Blowing out trick candles
And it's not my birthday,
Nor the suns or the flowers.
I don't want prayers or pity
I indulge in it.
Because it's better than the doctor's remedy
Which leaves me blank.
No writing, no reading, no words.
Blank.

Sadness is better than Xanax.

HERIDA ABIERTA (HAYNAKU)

(from Gloria Anzaldua's *Borderlands*, her words, remixed)

Borderland
vague undetermined
place. Emotional residue.

Atravesados
live here
squint eyed mongrels

Mestizos
bracero, mojado
cucaracho culture courageous.

Faceless nameless invisible
Hey, Cucaracho!
cornered

Cactus
Mother's milk
Moon goddess sacrifice

who
possessed both
light and underworld

vegetated
hibernated remained
in stasis, idled

I
cultivate needles
nettles, razor sharp

Chicanos
blame themselves
terrorize ourselves, unconsciously

Cágandome
buscando lugares

HOMECOMING

I live in the antithesis
of myself. I am confronted
with ghosts in the wind that whisper
I will never know my home again.
The ghosts pray.
Padre Nuestro en el viento.
I don't want to take pictures
with the water tower.
I want your roads again,
your citrus groves,
your canales, quelite, mesquite,
the fields of sorgo, the cara cara,
the egrets with green eyes that pierce me.
That indigo snake, urraca, mala mujer by the
Rotel. Homeless men won't even hang out there now.

You have wrecked me home.
There is no homecoming
for tourists.

Steps to Surviving the Darkness

1. Buy an iPad because your kids will wonder where mommy is.
2. Cook a lot of stuff. People will eat and you don't have to tell them you've been crying.
3. Make sure that you use white onions because they make you cry the most.
4. Cover the mirrors with rebozos hand woven by women in Chiapas.
5. Talk to the dead. Their pictures are on your altar for a reason.
6. Sing an old alabanza that your Grandmother made you record on an old-fashioned tape recorder when you were 6.
7. Every picture in your childhood photo album tells a story. Listen.
8. Elvis Presley and Amalia Mendoza sound better during this time. Gracias a YouTube.
9. You have 3 days to email a note to yourself saying...
   Subject: You will survive. Body: Please don't sing karaoke.
10. Remember a shadow isn't a shadow without tequila.

LATELY

there are no sunsets
Clouds blow in from the southeast
Not rain clouds but whispering clouds
that may or may not be smoke

Lately fewer birds sing on the deformed oak branches
The tips of the oaks are still bare

I line up rocks on the phantom railroad tracks
I watch people stretch to train for triathlons
I listen to radio shows

I forgot how to dance bachata

Lately the silence reminds me of all the people
who have come and gone
who have lived in my home
who never said thank you

Lately I have looked
at myself in pictures and don't recognize
my own smile

Lately you are too far away
I watch you breathe through binoculars
Your belly grows, shrinks

There is tequila in the freezer
and it sucks there is only wine and no beer.

A Meditation
(for Gun Appreciation Day)

Pen as weapon
Pen as pleasure
Pen as liberator
Pen as enemy------penemy
Pen as absolution
Pen as possibility
Pen as priest
Pen as penance
Pen as knife
Pen as blood
Pen as wings
Pen as holy, holy, holy
Pen as pendeja
Pen as braggadocio
Pen as revolution
Pen as mistake
Pen as hallucinogen
Pen as reporter
Pen as curandera
Pen as partera
Pen as perdición
Pen as maldición
Pen as progress
Pen as metronome
Pen as paint
Pen as fallacy
Pen as corruption

Pen as pecado
Pen as séance
Pen as bang bang

MÁS O MENOS

One more Juana-be
is going to out-Mexican me today

So I burn incense and pray

One more güerita
is going to get
Coatlicue tattooed
on her thigh today

under my breath
I let out a Diosito Santo
and sip Nescafé

One more Juanita come lately
is going to teach my literature today
write her dissertation on hegemony cricket
and I say
eh mañana
I will get my way one day

(Siesta)

Did I just colonize myself?

Es que aquí en la colonia de mi corazón
me siento bien agusto

and I know
my cultura is bien de aquellas
que hasta las güeritas want to be like nosotras

and I say
¿por qué no?

Mi Raza es su Raza

BETRAYAL

I eat it for breakfast.

Beautiful. I have given birth and it's not.

Bent. The truth. Bent. My back. Bent.

Beatific. Pray to buzzards. They live off my carcass.
The stench of rotting livers and spleens.

Bitch.
Yes? You called?

Betrayal. I eat if for lunch. You deliver.
The tip is on the bedstand.
Bedstand. Bed. Be. Bounty.
But you haven't written a poem and I forgot how to draw.
Been caught lying. Been caught dealing.
Been caught and been better. Really.

Betrayal is better for dinner with a crisp moscato.
It's easy to swallow with sweet. Brie on the side fried.
Been caught being. Be.

The oak tree will shed its leaves in a day.
I can blame it all on my allergies. These aren't tears.

Bitch? Me? Do you think it befits me?
Betrayal. Beautiful. Bent.

The tip is on the bedstand.

H.E.B DREAMS

La Llorona met with Ginsberg. She finally had time to read after she left the children to die in the bathtub. Left. She never believed she did it on purpose. She couldn't hear them fussing and fighting in the bathtub over her iPod that played "Bad Romance" on repeat.

They met at HEB a local grocery store and sampled quesadillas made with goat cheese and habanero which made Llorona's eyes water. Laura, he called her. "Laura, why did you drown your children? Do you have any remorse?"

She said, "No. I have decided to accept loss forever."

Ginsberg looked around in his hungry fatigue. This grocery store had a million piñatas, bread of all colors. Candles of all saints and sizes. He missed Walt more than ever. This woman was a weepy girl, crying over everything from the price of cigarettes to the out-of-season corn. "So, what do you want to discuss?"

La Llorona straightened her shawl. Women recognizing her would do a double take and kiss their babies. They vowed no matter how much they loved Lady Gaga, they would pay attention to their babies as they bathed.

"Well, I've been reading your work, all I can borrow from our crappy library anyway. I don't like Howl. Everyone says it's your greatest poem. America, now that's your best, hands down."

Ginsberg was too busy staring at the checkers. The boys these days esp. at this HEB were so out, they were never in.

"I am in agreement with you," he said, brushing her off. He pulled out his iPhone to take a picture of a boy he would try to impress and take home to show his amazing collection of Time Magazine that dated way before this boy's mother was even born.

OBSESSED WITH TIME MAGAZINE
(BASED ON PICS OF THE WEEK)
After Allen Ginsberg

Vinyl masks on fire smell like revolution
always keep an extra one in case of an effigy emergency

As a child, playing with military warfare flashcards
proved to pass the time on a Saturday

Hope at Westpoint:
We can ask and tell if we want to and no one will fire us

Boats on dry river beds don't mean anything to
those who don't believe in global warming

No matter how you put it
famine surpasses time

Blood pools on a cobblestone street
Eid al-Adha marks the end of the Hajj

Carrying coal in Kabul
a man does what he must to keep warm

Queens love nothing more than seeing women
of the Commonwealth dress like golden bees when she is the
flower

Horton heard who and it frightened him so

Collegers challenge Oppidians and no one wins
Except for Hulkmania. You can't lose with Hulkmania

Bollywood theatres are as lush as their movies
A lone man in an empty theatre is addicted to the song and show,
the glimmer and glamour

When soldiers cry a dove dies.

Prayers fill the Hira cave,
prayers that can save the world

Laplanders always take cliché walks in snow-covered evergreen
forests
at Christmas time with authentic huskies and real reindeer

Obama walks the Great Wall of China oblivious to the wall being
built here on our border. Border, schmorder

Remember that when a soldier dies
all soldiers cry

Flat screens with queens always look like an infinite mirror

Tear gas canisters look like whippits
except this is no laughing matter

If a Mapuche Indian wants his land back, he must be reminded that
lumber is more important than blood

But you can always make a trip to a Beaujolais Noveau spa for a
break from all the madness
And circus bears on hockey skates take the edge off of
Globalization

Goddamn communists. It's always the Russians, the Russians and
will always be the Russians
Except this time they're ISIS

But a circus bear is a circus bear
And Boujelais Noveau is only available during the holidays

TACUACHE FRIEND

Tacuache
Hold back the dawn for me
You did it for Xbalanque
I need this night to last one more day

Tacuache
I can't stand the sight of you
What with your two vaginas
Misplaced member
Hairless tail
Opposable toes
But what would you think of me
I'm a horrible mother
I have no pouch or patience

Tacuache
In the valley you steal grapefruits
Inhabiting the underworld of wooden frame homes
And drainage pipes
Walking on electric tight ropes
Best seen by natives as road kill on FM88

Tacuache
Mesoamerican myth hero
The four quarters
Moon
Maguey
Dismemberment
Regeneration

Almost a God for the Zapotec
Made the rivers crooked for the Mazatec

Tacuache
This is for you
Fierce fighter
Thief of fire
Fight the migra
We'll deify you again

CROSS ROADS

(in four parts)

1.

Out the window
I've thrown a lemon
into the grapefruit grove
at the Y on highway 107

Here I have left envidia
que la gente me tiene
porque así son
envidiosos

out the window
all the negative energy
everyone who has cursed me
everyone que se ponen celosos
porque soy muy chingona
¡ah! no te creas

Aquí at the crossroads
Me persigno

En el nombre de
poesía
antepasados
y el futuro

when standing at the crossroads
¡cuidado!
Porque dicen que aquí se aparece la Llorona
I've heard stories about spirits who can't find rest
Don't know which way to go, which direction.

2.

La Frontera is my crossroads.

Which direction should I face?

I invoke all directions—

To the east–I invoke Yemaya!

To the West—The peregrine falcon, a cara cara

To the North—an evergreen wind

To the South,
To the South
To the South—

I invoke the struggle
I invoke hunger pains
I invoke resistance
I invoke amnesia
I invoke the ancestors

I invoke a Saturday listening to Esterio Mar, Rocio Durcal
I invoke Amalia Mendoza's tear-stained voice
I invoke Coatlique
I invoke the zopilote
I invoke confession
I invoke nightmares rooted in ventricles
I invoke fault lines, we balance and tether
I invoke my shed skin, I sew together prosthetic poetics
I invoke the indigenous woman to lick my wounds and patch me
up to break again
I invoke La Virgen
I invoke Xanax to numb the awareness of violence and severed
heads
I invoke street vendors drunkenly speaking Nahuatl, crying
conquest tears
I invoke el vietre inconsolable
I invoke squatting and pissing
in seatless toilets in alley bars
I invoke dulce de calabaza, soda de tamarindo
I invoke a dusty Saturday and milanesa con aguacate
with a side of Los Cadetes de Linares
I invoke caguamas de Canta Blanca and trannies
dancing tropical

I invoke

3.

She burns sage
my hair soaks the smoke.
On my hands
I've smudged an x of ash.

Diosa Gloria,

I spread out my arms
My legs.

My body is a crossroads.
I've survived. I've survived.
Congratulations to me!
I thrive.

4.

The wall has not split me into.

I am all directions.

MENUDO IN A CAN

Menudo in a Can, Man!!
Menudo in a can
And tamales
And pico de gallo in a jar
Instant Mexican rice
Fideo to go
Carnitas de Puerco at the Stripes
And frozen enchiladas!
Barbacoa every day?

We don't need Buelita anymore
Because she's dead anyway
And she never told us how she made
The mole.
The masa is premade
And we can buy tortillas ready for the comal.
No need to knead!

Lotería shower curtains and plates
 Frida on my bracelet
Coyoxachui on my t-shirt
Che Guevarra on my socks.
The word "Chula" printed on my chones.
Popocateptl tapestries
Baby Abuelita dolls that sing to your baby
Cantiflas posters,
Don Pedrito Jaramillo candles,
 Virgen Beach towels?

Our cultura is mainstream now.
Just add water and stir.

AFTER "JUSTIFY MY LOVE"

(RGV Version)

I want to kiss you in Las Milpas
I wanna do ya in La Grulla
I want to hold your hand in Monte Alto
I want to run naked cuando llueve in San Carlos
I want to make love by a tinaco

You did this to me
So what are you gonna do?

Wanting (menudo)
Needing (a nap)
Waiting
For you

Declara tu amor

I want to eat Tacos de Reynosa with you
No quiero ser tu abuela
Ni quiero ser tu hermana
I just want to be your lover, con safos

Tell me your dreams
Are they about Cantinflas
Tell me your stories
It's ok if you went to juvi
I'm not afraid of your back child support

I wanna be your Ruca
I wanna be your Vieja

I want you——
Declara tu amor

Dear God,

I wrote to you yesterday, but you have the odd habit of writing back to me in suicide notes. I searched for you and my credit card, but both appear to be misplaced. Your presence is in my early tequila sunrise and my late night cap to erase the pain of mortality. I prayed to the moon, to the sun, to the butterfly that was lost in the weeds. I prayed to the cat that sleeps all day and plays with bottle caps at night. Fichera, I named her. I prayed to Facebook. I tweeted a message to a goddess I met at Metropolis on Goth Night. She wore Doc Martens. She was my ghost.

There is a God, I know there is: there is a God who gave me the job of my dreams and children when I thought my womb was barren. There is a God, I believe, because the man I love loves me and holds me in the morning, his warm breath on my neck reminding me I am alive. There is a God and he lives, she lives, somewhere all of my ancestors feast on peace. There is a God, but right now...right now...this very instant, there is a God in my heart roaring like a lion to remind it to keep beating. To keep beating. To keep beating.

To keep being Beat.

LLORONA R.I.P.

Too many sightings, too many nights spent in the outskirts of Monte Alto, La Villa, San Carlos, Hargill, afraid to hear you wail while I made out with boys I didn't love in the back seat of a crappy car. All the frightened drives down back roads, hoping I won't see your soiled shawl floating in the August wind, your horse mouth agape, desperate pathetic woman who couldn't handle her shit. I've made you my contemporary, you've been to H.E.B. You worked at Barnes with me, we shelved books and I would see you crack a smile when toddlers played with trains. We went to the gay bar, danced to Bad Romance. I tried to canonize you and made homemade soy candles that smelled like lavender and manzanilla to burn in your honor. I washed your hair, held your hand, let you sleep in the futon in the office while I wrote 25-page papers about infanticide. You crossed the border, were deported, never had children. You had an affair with a young poet who wrote haikus for you. You became Chavela Vargas, Frida Kahlo, Selena. You're a Halloween costume I wore when I was pregnant. Yelling at the white children in my quaint gringolandia neighborhood, "¡Mis hijos!" Some blonde kid asked, "Who are you supposed to be?" I looked at him with my hollowed-out eyes and said, "I drowned my children because they wanted candy!" After my post-partum depression-- kissed my newborn girl, those rose cheeks on a pink baby, held her all night, sobbing for my diseased father. Almost drowned that 10-lb baby in my tears but she floated.

You won't scare me anymore. You are Día de los Muertos. You are canned menudo. You won't haunt me anymore. Prozac killed you. Celebrex contained you. I bury you today. I bury these tears away.

author biography

ERIKA GARZA-JOHNSON grew up in Elsa, Texas, and has been reading and performing her poetry in the Río Grande Valley since 2001. Garza-Johnson received her MFA in Creative Writing from the University of Texas Pan American. A writing instructor at South Texas College, she lives in McAllen with her husband and her two children. She has served as the poetry editor for *New Border Voices: An Anthology* (Texas A&M University Press, 2014) and *¡Juventud! Growing Up on the Border* (VAO Publishing, 2013). Additionally, her poetry has been featured online in *La Bloga, Con Tinta*, and *Poets Against SB 1070*. Her work has also appeared in *Texas Observer* and *Border Senses*.

other titles from

VAO PUBLISHING

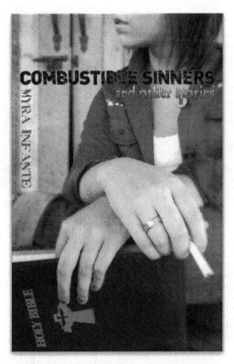

Combustible Sinners and Other Stories
by Myra Infante
ISBN: 9780615556703

Lissi Linares is a pastor's daughter whose love for others contrasts with her fear of eternal damnation. Little Jasmine "Jazzy Moon" Luna is determined to save Jesus from being crucified. Naida Cervantes hides a brutal secret behind shapeless, florid dresses. Hermana Gracie tries to set her son up with a good Christian girlfriend, only to make a surprising discovery. Zeke wants a new guitar and Ben wants a cool girlfriend, but what they find as migrant workers in Arkansas changes their desires. These individuals and others try to negotiate the often rocky intersection of faith and culture in seven independent but intertwining tales that explore life in an evangelical Christian, Mexican-American community. Frank, funny and heart-breakingly real, this volume explores themes of identity, culture, religion and sexuality in the context of a little-known subset of Hispanic culture.

¡Juventud! Growing up on the Border
Edited by René Saldaña, Jr., and Erika Garza-Johnson
ISBN: 9780615778259

Borders are magical places, and growing up on a border, crossing and recrossing that space where this becomes that, creates a very special sort of person, one in whom multiple cultures, languages, identities and truths mingle in powerful ways. In these eight stories and sixteen poems, a wide range of authors explore issues that confront young people along the US-Mexico border, helping their unique voices to be heard and never ignored.

Featuring the work of David Rice, Xavier Garza, Jan Seale, Guadalupe García McCall, Diane Gonzales Bertrand, and many others.

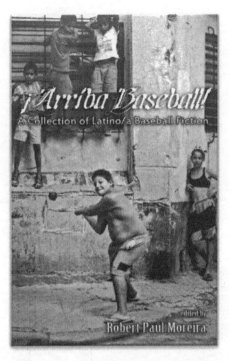

¡Arriba Baseball! A Collection of Latino/a Baseball Fiction
Edited by Robert Paul Moreira
ISBN: 9780615781839

From Dodger Stadium to the Astrodome, from the Río Grande Valley to
Chicago, from Veracruz to Puerto Rico, from high-school teams to stickball
in the streets, from the lessons of fathers to the excited joy of daughters,
from massive cheering in the stands at Wrigley Field to the dynamics of
family and community echoing on the diamond, these fifteen stories use the
sport of baseball to explore geographical, cultural and dream-like spaces
that transcend traditional notions of the game and transform it into a
universal yet wholly individual experience.

Featuring the work of Dagoberto Gilb, Norma Elia Cantú, Nelson Denis,
Christine Granados, René Saldaña, Jr., and many more.

Mexican Bestiary | *Bestiario Mexicano*
by David Bowles and Noé Vela
ISBN: 9780615571195

Who protects our precious fields of corn? What leaps from the darkness when you least suspect it? Which spirit waits for little kids by rivers and lakes? From the ahuizotl to the xocoyoles—and all the imps, ghosts and witches in between—this illustrated bilingual encyclopedia tells you just what you need to know about the things that go bump in the night in Mexico and the US Southwest.

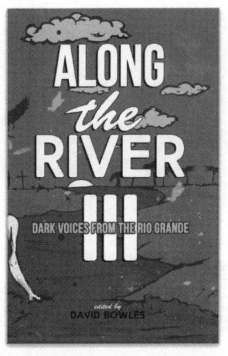

Along the River III: Dark Voices from the Río Grande
Edited by David Bowles
ISBN: 978-0615956183

The third anthology in the *Along the River* series.

When the sun sets on the Río Grande Valley, all manner of dark voices begin to croak, snarl and wail. Come explore the black shadows amidst the mesquite and palm trees down at the water's edge…just have a care not to fall (or be pulled) into the current.

Featuring the short story "Niño" by Álvaro Rodríguez.

FLOWERSONG BOOKS nurtures essential verse from the border-lands. A division of VAO Publishing, the imprint is named for the Nahuatl phrase *in xōchitl in cuīcatl*—literally "the flower, the song," a kenning for "poetry."

VAO Publishing is a division of the 501(c)(3) non-profit Valley Artist Outreach. Our mission is to promote both the voices of writers in the Río Grande Valley and the literacy of Hispanics in general. To achieve these goals, we are implementing a multi-tiered strategy:

- editing an annual anthology of local talent (*Along the River* is the name of this series)
- publishing a small number of titles by Valley authors (or by authors whose work would appeal to readers in the Valley) each year
- procuring top-notch authors to edit anthologies of established and upcoming writers whose work has special relevance to the Río Grande Valley
- providing creative writing workshops to aspiring local writers
- conducting writing contests for elementary and secondary children

Made in the USA
Charleston, SC
23 December 2015